Giannis Antetokounmpo

BY NORA GARDINER

Please visit our website, www.enslow.com. For a free color catalog of all our high-quality books, call toll free 1-800-398-2504 or fax 1-877-980-4454.

Library of Congress Cataloging-in-Publication Data

Names: Gardiner, Nora, author.
Title: Giannis Antetokounmpo / Nora Gardiner.
Description: New York : Enslow Publishing, [2022] | Series: Junior Bios | Includes index.
Identifiers: LCCN 2021021642 | ISBN 9781978525283 (Library Binding) | ISBN 9781978525269 (Paperback) | ISBN 9781978525276 (Set) | ISBN 9781978525290 (eBook)
Subjects: LCSH: Antetokounmpo, Giannis, 1994--Juvenile literature. | African American basketball players--Greece--Biography--Juvenile literature. | Basketball players--Greece--Biography--Juvenile literature. | Milwaukee Bucks (Basketball team)--History--Juvenile literature. | National Basketball Association--History--Juvenile literature. | Basketball--United States--History--Juvenile literature.
Classification: LCC GV884.A56 G37 2022 | DDC 796.323092 [B]--dc23
LC record available at https://lccn.loc.gov/2021021642

First Edition

Published in 2022 by
Enslow Publishing
29 E. 21st Street
New York, NY 10010

Copyright © 2022 Enslow Publishing

Designer: Deanna Paternostro
Editor: Kate Mikoley

Photo credits: Cover, p. 1 (Giannis Antetokounmpo) Dylan Buell/Contributor/Getty Images Sport/Getty Images; cover, p. 1 (photo frame) Aleksandr Andrushkiv/Shutterstock.com; marble texture used throughout HardtIllustrations/Shutterstock.com; lined paper texture used throughout Mtsaride/Shutterstock.com; watercolor texture used throughout solarbird/Shutterstock.com; p. 5 Pool/Pool/Getty Images Sport/Getty Images; p. 5 (inset) Stacy Revere/Contributor/Getty Images Sport/Getty Images; pp. 7, 9 Mike Stobe/Stringer/Getty Images Sport/Getty Images; p. 11 Orlando Sentinel/Contributor/Tribune News Service/Getty Images; p. 13 Richard Lautens/Contributor/Toronto Star/Getty Images; p. 14 PIERRE-PHILIPPE MARCOU/Staff/AFP/Getty Images; p. 15 Elsa/Staff/Getty Images Sport/Getty Images; p. 17 Kevork Djansezian/Stringer/Getty Images Sport/Getty Images; p. 19 MediaNews Group/Boston Herald via Getty Images/Contributor/MediaNews Group/Getty Images.

All rights reserved. No part of this book may be reproduced in any form without permission in writing from the publisher, except by a reviewer.

Printed in the United States of America

Some of the images in this book illustrate individuals who are models. The depictions do not imply actual situations or events.

CPSIA compliance information: Batch #CWENS22: For further information contact Enslow Publishing, New York, New York, at 1-800-542-2595.

Find us on

Contents

Greek Beginnings 4

Street Sales and Sports 6

The Draft 8

The Big Milwaukee Move 10

Rookie on the Court 12

Whiz Kid 14

Top of the League 16

MVP Challenges 18

Champ at Last 20

Giannis's Timeline 21

Glossary 22

For More Information 23

Index 24

Words in the glossary appear in **bold** type
the first time they are used in the text.

Greek Beginnings

There are many reasons NBA All-Star Giannis Antetokounmpo is known as the "Greek Freak." First of all, he's from Greece. Perhaps more importantly, he's a freak—a great player—on the court.

But his basketball skills mean more to him than just the fame and fortune of the NBA. He has used his success to make his family's life better.

FACTS BEHIND THE FIGURE

Giannis's full name is pronounced: YAH-nihs ahn-teh-toh-KOON-po.

GIANNIS IS ONE OF FIVE BROTHERS. TWO OF HIS BROTHERS HAVE ALSO PLAYED IN THE NBA: THANASIS AND KOSTAS.

Giannis was born December 6, 1994, near Athens, Greece. His parents were **undocumented immigrants** from Nigeria who came to Greece in 1991.

Street Sales and Sports

Giannis's parents had trouble finding work since they weren't Greek **citizens**. Growing up, Giannis and his brothers were always worried their parents would be sent back to Nigeria. Often, the brothers would have to work so their family could buy food and pay for their home. They sold sunglasses, watches, toys, and more on the streets.

The brothers were also talented at sports. Giannis liked playing soccer. Thanasis convinced him to try basketball too. Soon, Giannis was practicing until midnight and showing some real skill.

WHEN GIANNIS STARTED TRYING BASKETBALL,
HE WASN'T VERY TALL YET AND DIDN'T KNOW HOW TO PLAY AT ALL!

7

The Draft

By the time Giannis was 16, he was one of the best basketball players in Greece. He played on a semi-**professional** team, and NBA **scouts** started to take an interest in him. Giannis signed a contract to play professionally in Spain for the 2013 season. Then, the NBA called.

In His Own Words
"From the time I started in basketball, my dream was to be a big star, to have a big future in basketball."

LATER, GIANNIS SAID HE DIDN'T THINK HE WAS QUITE READY TO PLAY IN THE NBA WHEN HE WAS DRAFTED.

In 2013, Giannis was **drafted** 15th by the Milwaukee Bucks. At just 18, he moved to Milwaukee, Wisconsin, with his parents and two younger brothers. Before they moved, the Antetokounmpo brothers finally became Greek citizens.

The Big Milwaukee Move

Milwaukee Bucks players and staff helped Giannis **acclimate** to life in the United States. They helped him buy clothes and get furniture for the apartment he shared with his family. They even taught him to drive! Before he even played his first game, this gave Giannis a feeling of belonging in Milwaukee.

On the court, too, Giannis had a lot to learn. He had to learn to work with his teammates, some of whom were a lot older than him!

During his first season, Giannis told his teammates: "I love Milwaukee! I'm going to be in Milwaukee 20 years!"

Rookie on the Court

Giannis played his first professional basketball game on October 13, 2013. But the Bucks went on to have one of the worst seasons in the **franchise's** history, winning only 15 games out of 82. Giannis didn't play much anyway. He averaged only 6.8 points, 1.9 assists, and 4.4 rebounds per game.

When he was drafted, Giannis was 6 feet 8.5 inches (2.04 m) tall. He grew in the year that followed and now measures 6 feet 11 inches (2.1 m)!

EVEN THOUGH HE PLAYED ON THE WORST TEAM IN THE NBA FOR THE 2013–2014 SEASON, GIANNIS WAS NAMED TO THE NBA ALL-ROOKIE SECOND TEAM.

Still, Giannis got experience playing on a professional team. He was also showing enough promise that he was called the "Greek Freak" for the first time.

13

Whiz Kid

As the 2014–2015 season started, Giannis and the Bucks faced a big change: a new coach in NBA legend Jason Kidd. Kidd began playing Giannis as a point guard, an uncommon position for someone so tall. Giannis still didn't score a lot, but it was clear he was improving in an exciting way.

FACTS BEHIND THE FIGURE

Giannis has played on Greece's national team, including during the **tournament** to enter the 2016 Summer Olympics.

GIANNIS TOOK PART IN THE SLAM DUNK CONTEST AT THE NBA ALL-STAR WEEKEND IN 2015.

The 2015–2016 season put Giannis in the spotlight. He became the main ball mover on the court for the Bucks. His dunks, long-range passes, and many triple-doubles made sports highlights all season.

15

Top of the League

As Giannis improved, so did the Bucks. The team's winning record in the 2016–2017 season came in part from Giannis showing how far he'd come. He made history as the first player in the NBA to ever be **ranked** in the top 20 for total points, assists, rebounds, blocks, and steals.

FACTS BEHIND THE FIGURE

In 2017, Giannis won the NBA's Most Improved Player award.

GIANNIS WAS A STARTER IN BOTH THE 2017 AND 2018 NBA ALL-STAR GAMES.

The following season, Giannis's play remained among the best in the NBA. He averaged a double-double with 26.9 points and 10 rebounds per game.

MVP Challenges

In 2018, NBA legend Magic Johnson said of Giannis: "He's going to be an MVP, a champion, this dude, he's going to put Milwaukee on the map and win them a championship." In the 2018–2019 season, Giannis did part of that: he was named the NBA's Most Valuable Player (MVP).

In His Own Words

"I think about where I was ... on the streets. and where I am today. able to take care of my kids and my grandkids and their grandkids. I'm not saying that in a cocky way or a disrespectful way. But it is a crazy story. isn't it?"

ON TWITTER, NBA LEGEND KOBE BRYANT HAD CHALLENGED GIANNIS TO WIN MVP DURING THE 2018–2019 SEASON. GIANNIS SET THAT GOAL AND ACHIEVED IT!

In 2020, NBA play was put on hold during the COVID-19 **pandemic**. When games began again, the Bucks lost to the Miami Heat in the playoffs. Still, Giannis was named Defensive Player of the Year! He also won MVP again.

19

Champ at Last

Giannis signed a new contract with Milwaukee in December 2020. It stated he would play for the Bucks for five more years! Giannis said he wanted to win a championship, and he wanted to do it with the Bucks.

Giannis took the Bucks to the playoffs. The Bucks beat the Phoenix Suns to win the NBA Championship in July 2021! Giannis scored 50 points and got 14 rebounds in the final game. He was named the NBA Finals MVP! What will he accomplish next?

FACTS BEHIND THE FIGURE

Giannis helped the Bucks win their first NBA Championship in 50 years!

Giannis's Timeline

DECEMBER 6, 1994: GIANNIS IS BORN IN GREECE.

2013: GIANNIS IS DRAFTED TO THE NBA BY THE MILWAUKEE BUCKS. HE IS GRANTED GREEK CITIZENSHIP.

OCTOBER 13, 2013: GIANNIS PLAYS IN HIS FIRST NBA GAME.

2014: HE STARTS PLAYING POINT GUARD UNDER COACH JASON KIDD.

2016–2017: GIANNIS BECOMES THE FIRST NBA PLAYER IN HISTORY TO RANK IN THE TOP 20 FOR TOTAL POINTS, ASSISTS, REBOUNDS, BLOCKS, AND STEALS.

2017: HE WINS THE NBA'S MOST IMPROVED AWARD.

2018–2019: GIANNIS IS NAMED THE NBA'S MVP.

2019–2020: GIANNIS IS NAMED THE NBA'S DEFENSIVE PLAYER OF THE YEAR AND MVP.

2021: THE BUCKS WIN THE NBA CHAMPIONSHIP. GIANNIS IS NAMED THE NBA FINALS MVP.

Glossary

acclimate To adapt to a new environment or situation.

citizen Someone who lives in a country legally and has certain rights.

draft To be selected from a pool of players entering a league.

franchise A professional sports team that is part of an organized league.

pandemic A time in which a disease spreads quickly and affects many people in an area or throughout the world.

professional Earning money for an activity.

rank To place in a position among a group of people who are being judged according to ability.

scout A person who searches for those with great skill in a sport.

tournament A series of contests testing the skill of many teams in the same league.

undocumented immigrant One who comes to a country to settle there illegally.

For More Information

Books

Bowker, Paul. *Giannis Antetokounmpo: Basketball Star*. Lake Elmo, MN: Focus Readers, 2019.

Fishman, Jon M. *Giannis Antetokounmpo*. Minneapolis, MN: Lerner Publications, 2019.

Websites

Giannis Antetokounmpo: Stats
www.nba.com/players/giannis/antetokounmpo/203507
Follow Giannis's stats on NBA.com.

Giannis Antetokounmpo: YouTube Channel
https://bit.ly/2CGrlVp
Visit Giannis's YouTube channel to get lots of behind-the-scenes information about the basketball superstar.

Publisher's note to educators and parents: Our editors have carefully reviewed these websites to ensure that they are suitable for students. Many websites change frequently, however, and we cannot guarantee that a site's future contents will continue to meet our high standards of quality and educational value. Be advised that students should be closely supervised whenever they access the internet.

Index

Antetokounmpo, Kostas, 5

Antetokounmpo, Thanasis, 5, 6

assists, 12, 16, 21

Bryant, Kobe, 19

Defensive Player of the Year, 19, 21

family, 4, 5, 6, 9, 10

Greece, 4, 5, 6, 8, 9, 14, 21

Johnson, Magic, 18

Kidd, Jason, 14, 21

Miami Heat, 19

Milwaukee Bucks, 9, 10, 12, 14, 15, 16, 18, 19, 20, 21

Miwaukee, Wisconsin, 9, 10, 11

Most Improved Player, 16, 21

Most Valuable Player (MVP), 18, 19, 20, 21

NBA All-Star Games, 17

Nigeria, 5, 6

Phoenix Suns, 20

playoffs, 19, 20

points, 12, 16, 17, 19, 21

rebounds, 12, 16, 17, 20, 21

Spain, 8

Toronto Raptors, 19